Cook Once Eat All Week Recipes

A Complete Cookbook of Delicious Make-Ahead Dish Ideas!

BY: Allie Allen

COOK & ENJOY

Copyright 2020 Allie Allen

Copyright Notes

Table of Contents

Introduction

Do you try to get everything done every day without success?

Do you have days when making a healthy dinner almost doesn't even cross your mind, till it's almost time to eat?

Do you enjoy having meals ready for your family, so you can serve them delicious and healthy foods that will benefit everyone?

Sure, some things can wait a while, like laundry and maybe dishes. But guilty feelings creep in if you feel you're not feeding your family well.

Making meals ahead will help you out. They'll free up time every day just by spending a few hours at once on a weekend day to prepare the meals and freeze them. It makes your life less stressful.

Now, you'll have dinners prepared and ready to heat on days when you'd be hard-pressed to find the time to prepare a full, hearty and healthy meal. Just open your freezer and grab a bag or plastic container of prepared food to reheat.

Some freezer meals take a bit of time to prepare at the start, but that time spent is SO worth it. Many make-ahead meals only take 15-20 minutes to put together, and you'll be saving time all week, just reheating them for your family. What could be better? Let's get cooking...

1 – Freezer Lime Cilantro Chicken

This is a delicious dinner that is frozen, then prepared in an Instant Pot. What a time saver! You can serve it in burrito bowls if you like, for a delicious meal.

Makes 6 Servings

Cooking + Prep Time: 45 minutes

Ingredients:

- 1 pound of chicken breast, skinless, boneless
- 1 cup of orange juice, fresh
- 1 cup of broth, chicken
- 2 limes, fresh, juice only
- 2 tsp. of garlic, minced
- 1/2 cup of cilantro leaves, chopped
- 1 can of drained, rinsed black beans
- 2 cups of corn, frozen
- 1 tbsp. of cumin, ground

Instructions:

1. Add the ingredients to large size freezer bag and label. Place in freezer.

2. To prepare, add frozen contents to Instant Pot. Sauté for five minutes, till liquid amount is about 1/4 cup. Cook for 10-12 minutes under high pressure. Allow 10 minutes to elapse for a natural pressure release. Serve.

2 – Make-Ahead Caramelized Onions

Learning the way to caramelize onions properly is the key to this dish. After you master the technique, you can use the method in many dishes.

Makes 1/2 cup +

Cooking + Prep Time: 1 hour 50 minutes

Ingredients:

- 2 peeled large onions, yellow
- 2 tbsp. of butter, unsalted
- Salt, kosher

Optional for pan: filtered water or chicken broth, low sodium

Instructions:

1. First, slice onions in halves through their root ends. Then, carefully use the tip of a knife to cut V-shaped notch in and around the root, removing it.

2. Place one onion half on cutting board, with root end facing you. Then, slice onion thinly lengthwise. Certainly, slices should be between 1/4" and 1/8" thick.

3. Repeat the same procedure on the rest of your halved onions.

4. Next, heat 2 tbsp. of butter in large pan on med. heat till it melts and sizzles. Add onions a couple handfuls at a time so they'll cook evenly. Stir while cooking till onions become soft and begin turning translucent, just a couple minutes. Stir several more handfuls in. Repeat the cooking and stirring till all onions have been added. Season with a bit of kosher salt.

5. Reduce the heat down to med-low. Continue cooking onions and stir frequently so they won't stick or become over-colored in small areas, till all are blonde in color, about 15 to 20 minutes. This is where you want them for soup.

6. If you want them more caramelized and softer for onion dips or patty melts, continue to cook and stir frequently till the onions are golden brown in color.

7. Allow the onions to cool in pan. Transfer to a lidded container. Chill. You can use them for up to a week.

3 – Freezer Smoked Sausage Pasta

Undoubtedly, this pasta dish is one you'll want to try. It tastes delicious when it is bubbly and hot from your oven, and the French-fried cheddar onions add a crunchy and cheesy taste.

Makes 6 Servings

Cooking + Prep Time: 50 minutes

Ingredients:

- 2 cups of penne pasta, uncooked
- 1 lb. of 1/4"-sliced sausage, smoked
- 1 1/2 cups of milk, 2%
- 1 x 10 3/4 oz. can of condensed, undiluted soup, cream of celery
- 1 1/2 cups of French-fried onions, cheddar
- 1 cup of mozzarella cheese shreds
- 1 cup of peas, frozen

Instructions:

1. Preheat the oven to 375F. Cook the pasta using instructions on package.

2. In large-sized skillet, brown the sausage on med. heat for five minutes. Drain the sausage.

3. In large-sized bowl, combine soup and milk. Stir in 1/2 cup of cheese, 1/2 cup of onions, then sausage and peas. Drain the pasta. Then, stir into the sausage mixture.

4. Transfer to lightly greased 13" x 9" casserole dish. Cover. Bake till bubbly, 20-30 minutes approximately. Then, evenly sprinkle with the rest of the cheese and onions. Leave uncovered and bake till cheese melts, three to five more minutes. Allow dish to cool.

5. Place meal in freezer container/s and freeze until needed. When ready to serve, microwave meal or pour it into a skillet to warm.

4 – Make-Ahead Cuban-Style Beans

This recipe was written to be doubled, tripled or even quadrupled for feeding a family for a few nights, rather than just one. You won't want to eat the same exact meal every night, so preparing two or three will give you some varieties when you're heating dishes up later in the week.

Makes 2 quarts +

Cooking + Prep Time: 3 hours 40 minutes

Ingredients:

- 1 lb. of dried beans, black, rinsed and picked through
- 1 bay leaf, medium
- 1 chopped onion, medium
- 1 bell pepper, green – remove ribs and seeds and chop finely
- 8 finely grated cloves of garlic
- 1 tbsp. of salt, kosher + extra as needed
- 1 tsp. of oregano, Italian or dried Mexican
- 1/4 cup of oil, olive
- Pepper, ground

Optional, for serving: tender-stemmed cilantro leaves

Instructions:

1. Bring 5 quarts of filtered water plus the beans, 1/4 cup of chopped onions, bay leaf, 1/4 cup of chopped peppers, 1 tbsp. of grated garlic, 1 tbsp. of kosher salt, 1/2 tsp. of oregano to boil in large-sized pot.

2. Reduce the heat level to med. Stir occasionally while cooking. Add additional heated water as needed till beans become tender and are fully covered by 1/4-inch of liquid, about two and a half hours. Discard the bay leaf.

3. Heat the oil in skillet on med-low. Add remainder of onions, along with oregano, bell peppers and garlic. Season as desired. Stir occasionally while cooking till onions are soft and starting to brown, 15 minutes. Stir them into the cooked beans.

4. These beans can be prepared up to three MONTHS ahead of time. Transfer them to a lidded container, then freeze until needed. Reheat to serve.

5 – Freezer Chicken Rolls

This recipe will actually make your mouth watering even as you prepare it. The rolled ham cheese inside chicken tastes great with pasta or rice.

Makes 6 Servings

Cooking + Prep Time: 30 minutes + 4 hours slow cooker time

Ingredients:

- 6 chicken breast halves, skinless, boneless
- 6 slices of ham, fully cooked
- 6 slices of cheese, Swiss
- 1/4 cup of flour, all-purpose
- 1/4 cup of Parmesan cheese, grated
- 1/2 tsp. of sage, rubbed
- 1/4 tsp. of paprika, smoked
- 1/4 tsp. of pepper, ground
- 1/4 cup of oil, canola
- 1 x 10 3/4-oz. can of undiluted, condensed soup, cream of chicken
- 1/2 cup of broth, chicken

Instructions:

1. Flatten the chicken till it is 1/4-inch thick. Top it with cheese and cooked ham. Then, roll them up and tuck in the ends. Secure them with toothpicks.

2. In shallow, medium bowl, combine the cheese, flour, paprika, sage ground pepper. Coat the chicken on each side. In large-sized skillet, add oil and brown the chicken on med-high.

3. Transfer mixture to large slow cooker. Combine the broth and soup and pour it over the chicken. Cover. Then, cook on the low setting for 4-5 hours, till chicken becomes tender. Remove the toothpicks.

4. To freeze for later, cool the chicken mixture and place in food storage freezer containers. When ready to prepare, thaw partially in the refrigerator overnight. The next day, heat through slowly in skillet till internal temp reads 165F.

6 – Make-Ahead Beans Farro

These beans taste more delicious because the cooking liquid is infused using aromatic ingredients like garlic and onions. The dish is seasoned liberally till it's almost salty.

Makes 4+ Servings

Cooking + Prep Time: 2 hours 55 minutes

Ingredients:

- 1 unpeeled halved onion, small
- 1 peeled carrot, medium
- 1 clove of garlic, smashed
- 3 cloves of garlic, chopped finely
- 1 1/2 cups of lima beans – soak overnight and drain
- 1 cup of spelt or farro – soak overnight and drain
- Salt, kosher
- 2 de-seeded, chopped chilies, Fresno
- 1/3 cup + 3 tbsp. of oil, olive
- 2 tbsp. of rosemary, chopped finely
- 8 oz. of bite-sized torn mushrooms, shiitake or maitake
- 2 tsp. of vinegar, red wine or sherry
- Pepper, freshly ground
- 4 room temperature egg yolks, large

Instructions:

1. Bring 14 cups of filtered water, along with beans, smashed garlic, carrots and onions to boil in pot. Lower the heat. Stir occasionally while simmering till beans become creamy but are still basically intact, about an hour and a half. Transfer the beans to bowl. Discard the smashed garlic, onions and carrots.

2. Return broth in same pot to boil. Add the farro. Lower heat. Stir occasionally while simmering till grains become tender, 25 minutes. Remove pot from the heat. Return the beans to their pot. Generously season using salt. Allow to sit for 15-18 minutes.

3. Cook 1/3 cup of oil, chopped garlic and chilies in skillet on med. heat. Stir them often, till the garlic turns golden, four minutes. Remove from the heat. Add rosemary and mix. Transfer the garlic-chile oil to small sized bowl. Use salt to season.

4. Wipe skillet out. Heat last 3 tbsp. of oil on med-high. Cook the mushrooms without stirring till the underneath sides have browned. Toss, then continue cooking and toss now and then till mushrooms are crisp and browned in many spots. Splash mushrooms with vinegar. Season as desired.

5. To make ahead, prepare stew without the mushrooms, garlic-chile oil and egg yolks, up to three days ahead of time. Allow it to cool, then cover with secure lid and chill. Reheat on serving day.

7 – Freezer Skillet Sausage Shrimp

This recipe serves two purposes: one meal for now, two more for later. The chicken broth and sausage/shrimp/rice mixture are frozen separately and thawed overnight before you cook them.

Makes 12 Servings

Cooking + Prep Time: 55 minutes

Ingredients:

- 2 x 2-lb. bags of raw shrimp, frozen
- 1/4 cup of oil, olive
- 2 tbsp. of butter, unsalted
- 4 cups of white rice, long-grain
- 1 chopped onion, large
- 4 1"-cut pieces of sausage links, precooked
- 1 chopped large bell pepper, green
- 2 tsp. of garlic, chopped finely
- 1 x 14 1/2-oz. can of tomatoes, diced, with juice
- Salt, kosher
- Pepper, black, ground
- 6 cups of broth, chicken

Instructions:

1. Divide frozen shrimp in three portions. 1st portion should be added to cold water in large-sized bowl, to thaw. 2nd and 3rd portions should be placed in separate, resealable large freezer food storage bags. Label them and place in freezer.

2. In a deep, large skillet, heat butter and oil on med-high. Add onions and rice. Stir occasionally while cooking till onions soften, five minutes or so. Add sausage, garlic and peppers. Stir while cooking till veggies soften, three to four minutes. Remove skillet from heat. Add and stir tomatoes their canned juice. Season as desired.

3. Transfer 2/3 of rice and veggie mixture to medium bowl. Allow it to cool. Add and stir 2 cups of chicken broth into rice in skillet.

4. To cook the 1st meal for tonight, bring rice mixture to boil. Then lower heat and cover. Simmer till rice becomes tender, 17-20 minutes. Drain thawed shrimp. Add to rice mixture and stir often while cooking on med. heat for five minutes or so, till shrimp are opaque.

5. To freeze the other two meals, divide remaining rice mixture in resealable, large freezer food storage bags. Pour 2 cups of broth in each bag. Then seal and label them. Place them in the freezer. Thaw one shrimp bag and one rice bag per meal overnight when you're ready to serve. Cook as you did in step 4 above.

8 – Make Ahead Lentil Cassoulet

This recipe offers you a rich and hearty lentil cassoulet without the typical hours needed to assemble and cook. You'll sub lentils for beans, and the lentils don't need to be presoaked.

Makes 8+ Servings

Cooking + Prep Time: 3 1/2 hours

Ingredients:

- 1/4 cup + 3 tbsp. of oil, olive
- 1 pound of 2"-torn mushrooms, wild
- 2 1/2 tsp. of salt, kosher
- 1 pound of 1" diagonal cut sausage, kielbasa
- 1 fennel bulb, large – chop bulb and fronds finely
- 1 chopped onion, large
- 2 peeled, chopped carrots, medium
- 2 chopped stalks of celery
- 8 cloves of garlic, sliced thinly
- 3 cloves of garlic, whole
- 1 tbsp. of thyme leaves, fresh
- 1 1/4 tsp. of Spanish paprika, smoked, hot
- 1/2 tsp. of crushed pepper flakes, red
- 3 tbsp. of tomato paste, double-concentrated
- 2 cups of lentils, green or black
- 1 x 2-inch torn baguette

Instructions:

1. Preheat the oven to 350F. In Dutch oven on med-high, heat 1/4 cup of oil till it smokes. Add mushrooms. Cook without stirring till the undersides are golden brown. Turn the mushrooms over. Cook without stirring till they brown on second side. Transfer mushrooms to plate.

2. Add 3 tbsp. of oil to the same Dutch oven. Add sausage in one layer. Reduce the heat level to med. Cook without stirring till sausage browns on underside. Turn the sausage over. Brown second side.

3. Add 1 tsp. of salt, sliced garlic, celery, carrots, onions and chopped bulb of fennel. Stir often while cooking till veggies soften. Add pepper flakes, thyme and paprika. Stir while cooking for a minute. Add the tomato paste. Stir occasionally while cooking till paste has turned a darker color and starts sticking to bottom of the pot.

4. Stir in 1 tsp. of salt, mushrooms and lentils into mixture. Add 8 cups of filtered water. Raise heat level to med-high. Bring to boil. Reduce the heat level down to low and cover the pot. Leave the lid askew a bit. Continue cooking and stir several times, till most liquid is absorbed, and stew has become thick, 25 to 30 minutes.

5. Pulse the bread in food processor till it forms coarse crumbs. Transfer them to rimmed cookie sheet in one even layer. Then drizzle with last 1/4 cup of oil and coat evenly. Bake till golden brown in color, a half hour or so. Remove them from the oven. Grate last 3 cloves of garlic finely over the breadcrumbs and toss, incorporating well. Add fronds of fennel. Scatter 1/2 breadcrumbs over the stew. Transfer the pot to your oven. Leave uncovered and cook till some breadcrumbs cook into stew and the stew bubbles around edges. 15 minutes or so. Scatter last of breadcrumbs over the stew. Cook till stew has become quite thick, 12-15 minutes.

6. To make ahead, allow to cool, then cover and chill the cassoulet. To reheat, place uncovered pan in 350F oven.

9 – Freezer Mini Meatballs

This is a wonderful recipe, whether you use the meatballs in stews or soups, or toss them in a bun for a meatball sub. They're easy to make and can be stored in the freezer for three months.

Makes 4 Servings

Cooking + Prep Time: 35 minutes

Ingredients:

- 1 lb. of beef, ground
- 1/4 cup of parsley, flat-leaf, chopped
- 1 tbsp. of garlic, chopped finely
- 1 tsp. of paprika, smoked
- Salt, kosher
- Pepper, ground

Instructions:

1. Preheat oven to 450F. In large mixing bowl, crumble beef. Mix in garlic, parsley, smoked paprika, 1 tsp. of kosher salt 1/2 tsp. of ground pepper.

2. Form beef mixture into 16 balls. Thread them on four skewers.

3. Preheat grill pan on med-high heat. Grill meatballs and turn while grilling, till they are barely cooked through, 8-10 minutes or so.

4. Drain meatballs on paper towels. Then place them in foil or food containers with airtight lids and put in freezer. Defrost and reheat as desired.

10 – Make-Ahead Chickpeas

Adding olive oil and lemon zest gives these chickpeas fuller flavor and brightness. It's a welcome addition to any meals during the week.

Makes 8+ Servings

Cooking + Prep Time: 2 hours

Ingredients:

- 1 pound of chickpeas, dried - soak overnight and drain
- 1 thinly sliced onion, medium
- 6 crushed cloves of garlic
- 2 lemon zest strips 3-inch x 1-inch
- 1/4 cup of oil, olive
- Salt, kosher
- Pepper, ground

Instructions:

1. Combine the onion, chickpeas, lemon zest, garlic, 1 pinch salt and oil in large-sized pot. Add two quarts of filtered water. Combine well. Bring to boil. Reduce the heat level to med-low and stir occasionally while simmering, replacing evaporated water, till chickpeas become tender, two hours. Season as desired and allow to cool.

2. To make ahead, prepare as described. Transfer to airtight container. Chill. Reheat when desired.

11 – Freezer Sausage Chicken Jambalaya

Jambalaya is a wonderful Creole dish. It's quite versatile, combining rice with other ingredients that may include green peppers, onions or tomatoes.

Makes 8 Servings

Cooking + Prep Time: 55 minutes

Ingredients:

- 1 tbsp. of oil, canola
- 2 lb. of 1 1/2"-cubed chicken thighs, skinless, boneless
- 1 lb. of 1"-cubed sausage, smoked
- 1 chopped large onion, white
- 1 chopped large bell pepper, green
- 1 cup of celery, chopped
- 3 minced cloves of garlic
- 2 bay leaves, medium
- 1 tbsp. of seasoning blend, Creole
- 1 tsp. of thyme, dried
- 1 tsp. of oregano, dried
- 2 cups of uncooked rice, converted
- 3 cups of broth, chicken
- 2 x 14 1/2-oz. cans of diced tomatoes, fire-roasted

Instructions:

1. Heat the oil in Dutch oven on med-high heat. Add sausage and chicken. Stir constantly while cooking till meats have browned on each side, 8-10 minutes. Remove meats and place on layers of paper towels. Use them to blot the meats.

2. Add the bell peppers, onions, celery, bay leaves, garlic, Creole seasoning blend, oregano and thyme to the hot drippings. Cook them on med-high till vegetables become tender, five to seven minutes. Add rice and stir. Cook till fragrant, three or four minutes.

3. Stir in the broth, chicken, sausage and tomatoes. Bring to boil on high heat. Cover and reduce the heat level to med. Stir occasionally while simmering, till rice becomes tender, 20-25 minutes.

4. Ladle jambalaya into small food storage containers with airtight lids. Place in the freezer. Reheat in microwave as desired.

12 – Make-Ahead Steamed Beets

This method of steam roasting, using a covered pan on high heat, is an excellent way to prepare beets. The liquid keeps them from becoming dried out.

Makes 4+ Servings

Cooking + Prep Time: 20 minutes

Ingredients:

- 4 lb. of scrubbed halved large beets, red
- 2 tbsp. of oil, olive
- Salt, kosher
- Pepper, ground
- 1 rosemary sprig, fresh /or 1 handful thyme, fresh

Instructions:

1. Preheat the oven to 425F. Toss beets in oil in 13-inch x 9-inch casserole dish. Season as desired. Add herbs and then 1/4 cup of filtered water. Use foil to cover the pan tightly, so steam can build up. Roast the beets till somewhat soft.

2. Remove beets from the oven. Allow them to cool in a covered pan, which loosens the skins a bit. Use paper towels to finish rubbing off the skins.

3. To make ahead, steam the beets as indicated. Allow to cool, then cover them and chill till needed.

13 – Easy Freezer Beef Vegetable Soup

Indeed, there are few things more comforting on cold winter days than beef veggie soup. This soup is frozen in individual serving bowls, so you can pop one in the microwave whenever you like.

Makes 8 Servings

Cooking + Prep Time: 45 minutes

Ingredients:

- 1 tbsp. of oil, olive
- 1 lb. of stew meat, lean, cubed
- 1 x 12-oz. pkg. of seasoning blend, frozen
- 2 minced cloves of garlic
- 2 x 32-oz. cartons of broth, vegetable
- 2 x 14 1/2-oz. cans of petite tomatoes, diced
- 2 cups of cut corn, frozen
- 1 cup of cut okra, frozen
- 1 cup of lima beans, frozen
- 1 cup of green beans, cut, frozen
- 1/2 tsp. of pepper, ground
- 1/2 tsp. of thyme, dried
- 1/2 cup of pasta, uncooked

Instructions:

1. Heat the oil in Dutch oven on med-high heat. Add the meat, seasoning and minced garlic. Stir often while cooking till meat has browned seasoning becomes tender, 8-10 minutes or so.

2. Stir in broth, corn, tomatoes, lima beans, green beans, okra, thyme and ground pepper. Bring the mixture to boil on med-high heat. Then reduce the heat level to low. Stir occasionally while simmering till veggies become tender, 15-20 minutes.

3. Add pasta and stir it in. Stir occasionally while cooking stew till pasta becomes tender, 10-12 minutes.

4. Spoon stew from Dutch oven into small food containers with airtight lids. Freeze and use as desired. Reheat in microwave till it's as hot as you prefer it.

14 – Make Ahead Silky Mashed Potatoes

These tasty mashed potatoes can be made and chilled to be used later in the week. Add a bit more butter and milk to make them velvety and smooth.

Makes 8+ Servings

Cooking + Prep Time: 1 hour 20 minutes

Ingredients:

- 4 pounds of scrubbed potatoes, medium
- Salt, kosher
- 2/3 – 1 cup of cream, heavy
- 2/3 – 1 cup of milk, whole
- 1 1/4 cups of butter, unsalted, cut in pieces
- 1/2 cup of sour cream, reduced fat
- Pepper, ground

Instructions:

1. Place the potatoes in large-sized pot. Add cold water sufficient to cover the potatoes by an inch. Add large handful kosher salt. Reduce the heat. Simmer till potatoes become tender, but don't let them turn crumbly, 30 to 40 minutes. Drain. Return the potatoes to still warm pot, removed from heat, to dry.

2. Heat 2/3 of a cup of cream and 2/3 of a cup of milk in small pan on med. heat till almost simmering. Reduce the heat level to low. Keep liquid warm till you're ready to add it to the potatoes.

3. Pass heated potatoes unsalted butter through a ricer into large-sized bowl. Season as desired. Mix with masher till the butter has melted and combined with potatoes.

4. While mixing, add warm cream mixture gradually into potatoes. Mix in the sour cream. Season as desired.

5. To make ahead, prepare as above. Allow potatoes to cool, then cover them and chill. Reheat on med-low while stirring frequently so they won't stick.

15 – Freezer Tomato Cheese Casserole

Actually, this is a wildly delicious dish that is still easy to make. Tomato lovers will gobble it up, and it's a simple way to use extra tomatoes from your garden if you want to substitute them for the canned tomatoes in the recipe.

Makes 8 Servings

Cooking + Prep Time: 55 minutes

Ingredients:

- 2 x 35-oz. cans of drained, chopped tomatoes, whole
- 1 cup of crackers, butter, crushed – reserve 4 tbsp. to top
- 1 1/3 cups of cheddar cheese shreds, sharp – reserve 4 tbsp. to top
- 2 tbsp. of melted butter, unsalted
- 1 finely chopped onion, small
- 2 beaten eggs, large
- 1 tsp. of salt, kosher
- 1/2 tsp. of basil, dried
- 1/2 tsp. of paprika, sweet

Instructions:

1. Preheat the oven to 350F.

2. Layer tomatoes in 2 x 8" square or round casserole dishes.

3. In medium bowl, stir remainder of ingredients together. Reserve 4 tbsp. of crackers 4 tbsp. of cheese shreds for the topping.

4. Spoon mixture over the tomatoes. Sprinkle the reserved cheese crackers on top.

5. Bake casserole dishes in 350F oven for 45-50 minutes, till golden brown in color.

6. Remove dishes from oven. Transfer casserole to individual sized food containers. Close with airtight lids. Freeze for up to two weeks and use when desired. Microwave till they are heated to your liking.

16 – Make Ahead Mixed Bean Bonanza

When you prepare these marinated beans, soak shallots in vinegar and coat them with oil to prevent oxidation. In this way, they can be kept and used later.

Makes 4 cups +

Cooking + Prep Time: 15 minutes

Ingredients:

- 1 finely chopped shallot
- 3 tbsp. of vinegar, white wine
- 1/2 cup of tender herbs, chopped finely, like chives, cilantro, parsley mint
- 1/3 cup of oil, olive
- 2 x 15-oz. cans of rinsed chickpeas, black-eyed peas, navy beans, cannellini beans or a mixture of them
- 1 tsp. of pepper flakes, hot
- Salt, kosher

Instructions:

1. First, combine vinegar and shallot in small-sized bowl. Allow to sit for five minutes.

2. Mix oil and herbs in larger bowl, to coat the herbs. Add red pepper and beans. Combine by tossing. Season as desired.

3. Then, add the shallot mixture to the bean mixture. Gently toss and combine.

4. To make ahead, prepare as above. Cover the mixture and chill till you're ready to use.

17 – Freezer Tuna Casserole

This is a creamy tuna noodle casserole, filled with the ingredients that make it a comfort food extraordinaire. Also, it is especially tasty when served with a side salad.

Makes 6 Servings

Cooking + Prep Time: 40 minutes

Ingredients:

- 7 oz. of egg noodles, dried

For the white sauce:

- 1/4 cup of butter, unsalted
- 1/4 cup of flour, all-purpose
- 3/4 tsp. of basil
- 3/4 tsp. of oregano
- A dash of thyme, fresh
- 1/4 tsp. of salt, kosher
- 3 1/2 cups of milk, 2% or skim

Main Ingredients:

- 1/2 cup of Parmesan cheese, freshly grated
- 1 cup of peas, frozen
- 2 x 6 1/2-oz. cans of drained, flaked tuna

Toppings:

- 2 tbsp. of melted butter, unsalted
- 1/3 cup of breadcrumbs

Instructions:

1. Preheat the oven to 350F. Grease 10" x 8" x 2" casserole dish lightly.

2. Combine breadcrumbs in melted butter with fork in small-sized bowl. Set bowl aside.

3. Cook the noodles using instructions on package till al dente. Drain.

4. Add water to small pot. Bring to boil and cook peas till barely tender.

5. In medium sized pot on med-low heat, melt 1/4 cup of unsalted butter. Whisk in the all-purpose flour, oregano, basil, kosher salt and thyme. Whisk milk in slowly, constantly stirring till the sauce has thickened.

6. Remove pot from the heat. Add Parmesan cheese and stir, combining well.

7. Fold in tuna, drained noodles and peas.

8. Pour mixture in casserole dish. Sprinkle topping on. Bake in 350F oven for 18-20 minutes, then let it sit in casserole dish for five minutes or so.

9. Transfer tuna casserole to six individual food containers. Close with airtight lids. Freeze until you're ready for them. Microwave on med. till warm to reheat.

18 – Make Ahead Slow Cooker Beef Sandwiches

This recipe packs big flavor into tasty sandwiches. You can keep the meat in your refrigerator for up to a week for quick sandwich-making.

Makes 6+ Servings

Cooking + Prep Time: 10 minutes + 8-10 hours of slow cooker time

Ingredients:

- 2 lb. of roast, beef
- 1 pkg. of salad dressing mix, Italian
- 1 x 14-oz. can of broth, beef, low sodium
- 1 x 12-oz. can of beer – or an extra can of low sodium beef broth
- 1 x 16-oz. jar of pepperoncini
- 6 dinner rolls, French

Instructions:

1. Pour broth, beer if using and 1/2 pepperoncini juice in slow cooker. Add beef. Sprinkle Italian dressing packet in. Cover. Then, cook on the low setting for eight to 10 hours.

2. Remove beef. Shred with two forks. Place beef back in slow cooker.

3. To make ahead, use 3 to 4 lb. roast and 1 pkgs. Italian dressing mixture and cook on the low setting for 12 hours. Place in airtight bowl and chill till ready to use.

19 – Freezer Bean Burritos

These burritos are prepared during the weekend, so you'll have great meals during your busy work week. Loaded with beans, tomatoes and cheese, they are filling and delicious.

Makes 8 Servings

Cooking + Prep Time: 55 minutes

Ingredients:

- 2 tbsp. of oil, olive
- Salt, kosher, as desired
- Pepper, black, ground, as desired
- 1 x 16-oz. can of beans, refried
- 8 x 8" tortillas, flour
- 1 cup of cheddar cheese shreds
- 1 cup of Monterey Jack shreds
- 2 diced tomatoes, Roma if available
- 1/4 cup of cilantro leaves, fresh, chopped

Instructions:

1. Preheat the oven to 400F. Oil cookie sheet lightly.

2. Spread refried beans down middles of flour tortillas. Top with both cheeses, then tomatoes, and cilantro last. Fold in the opposite sides of tortillas. Roll up. Place on cookie sheet with the seam sides facing down. Cover burritos.

3. Bake burritos in 400F oven till heated fully through, 12-16 minutes.

4. To make ahead, cover baked burritos with foil or cling wrap. Freeze in heavy duty zipper top plastic bag. When reheating, use microwave to heat burrito for four to six minutes and turn when half done.

20 – Make Ahead Beef Stew

Beef stew is the perfect dish for cold winter nights. It's especially popular for game day dinners and parties.

Makes 8+ Servings

Cooking + Prep Time: 3 1/4 hours

Ingredients:

For stew

- 3 tbsp. of oil, olive
- 1 tbsp. of butter, unsalted
- 2 pounds of stew meat, beef
- Salt, kosher
- Pepper, ground
- 1 diced onion, medium
- 3 minced garlic cloves
- 4 oz. of tomato paste, no salt added
- 4 cups of beef broth, low sodium
- A few dashes of Worcestershire sauce
- 1/2 tsp. of sugar, granulated
- 4 peeled, diced carrots, whole
- 2 peeled, diced turnips
- 2 tbsp. of parsley, minced

Instructions:

1. Season stew meat with kosher salt ground pepper.

2. Heat oil in heavy, large pot on med-high. Add the butter. When it has melted, brown 1/2 stew meat till outside has browned nicely. Remove meat from pot and transfer to plate.

3. Add remainder of meat to pot. Brown it as well. Remove to same plate. Set meat plate aside.

4. Add garlic onions to pot. Stir and coat in brown bits from pot bottom. Cook for two minutes. Add tomato paste. Stir into onions and cook for two minutes more.

5. Add beef broth and constantly stir. Add sugar and Worcestershire sauce. Add beef back to pot. Cover. Reduce heat level to low. Leave lid on pan and simmer for 1 1/2 to 2 hours.

6. Add carrots and turnips to pot. Stir and combine well. Place lid back on pot. Allow to simmer for 1/2 hour more. Sauce should be thick. Thin with broth if desired.

7. When turnips and carrots become tender, add minced parsley. Season as desired.

8. To make ahead, prepare as above. Place in airtight container and chill. Reheat when desired.

21 – Freezer Sweet Potato Onion Wraps

This is such a handy way to prepare some lunches for the work week. Just roast the veggies during the spare time over the weekend, assemble them and stock in the freezer till you're ready to use them.

Makes 8 Servings

Cooking + Prep Time: 2 hours 25 minutes

Ingredients:

- 6 tbsp. of oil, olive
- 3 peeled, cubed sweet potatoes, large
- 3 de-stemmed, 1/4" sliced portobello mushrooms, large
- 1 pint of halved tomatoes, grape
- 2 thinly sliced, large onions, yellow
- 2 tbsp. of water, filtered
- 8 tortillas, whole-wheat, large
- 1/2 cup of pesto, basil
- 3/4 cup of Parmesan cheese, grated
- Salt, kosher
- Pepper, ground

Instructions:

1. First, arrange two oven racks to divide oven in thirds. Preheat to 400F.

2. Toss sweet potatoes in 3 tbsp. oil 1 tsp. salt. Arrange in one layer on two rimmed cookie sheets. Roast and stir when halfway done till potatoes have browned around edges and are tender, 35 minutes or so. Cool for five minutes +/-, and transfer sweet potatoes to large-sized plate. Reserve cookie sheets.

3. Next, toss mushrooms with 1 1/2 tbsp. oil 1/2 tsp. kosher salt. Place in one layer on rimmed cookie sheet. Toss tomatoes with 1/2 tbsp. oil. Arrange with cut side facing up on second cookie sheet. Roast in 400F oven for 12-15 minutes and stir mushrooms halfway through. Allow to cool on cookie sheets.

4. Heat last 1 1/2 tbsp. of oil in large sized skillet on low heat till it shimmers. Add onions and 1/2 tsp. of kosher salt. Stir every 10 minutes while cooking till onions are deeply browned and soft, a total of about 40 minutes cooking time. Add water and deglaze pan. Allow moisture to simply cook off.

5. Place tortillas on pieces of foil on your work surface. Spread 1 tbsp. pesto on each. Add 1/2 cup of sweet potatoes. Top them with two or three slices of mushrooms and 1 tbsp. each Parmesan cheese, onions and tomatoes. Roll up tightly and roll in foil pieces. Freeze in zipper top plastic bags. Reheat when desired in toaster oven in foil for 10 minutes then unwrapped for five minutes more.

22 – Make Ahead Roasted Chicken with Potatoes

This chicken dish is versatile and filled with proteins that you can use all week long. After a couple of nights of hot chicken dishes, try the cold chicken salad.

Makes 1 chicken

Cooking + Prep Time: 1 1/2 hour

Ingredients:

- 6 tbsp. of oil, olive
- 4 minced cloves of garlic, large
- 4 cloves of garlic, whole
- 2 tbsp. rosemary, chopped finely + 2 rosemary sprigs
- Salt, coarse
- Pepper, ground
- 2 fresh lemons, zest only
- 1 quartered lemon, fresh
- 1 x 4-lb. +/- chicken, whole
- 2 lb. of potatoes, baby, new
- 2 tbsp. of Parmesan cheese, grated

Instructions:

1. Preheat the oven to 400F. Place long chicken twine piece in bowl of filtered water. Remove giblets. Pat chicken dry using paper towels.

2. In small sized bowl, combine garlic, oil rosemary with 1-2 dashes each of kosher salt ground pepper.

3. Next, remove 1/2 mixture to separate, small-sized bowls. Mix lemon zest in one bowl.

4. Set chicken with breast side facing up in large-sized roasting pan. Liberally sprinkle chicken cavity as desired. Stuff garlic cloves, rosemary sprigs and lemon quarters inside chicken. Tie chicken legs up using twine. Tuck tips of wings under bird.

5. Then, rub oil-lemon mixture over chicken. Sprinkle as desired.

6. Toss potatoes with parmesan cheese and remainder of oil in large-sized bowl. Season well as desired. Place around chicken in roasting pan.

7. Lastly, roast for about an hour and a half till meat thermometer show 180F internal temperature. Then, let chicken rest for 10 to 15 minutes, then carve. Freeze in large zipper top bag. Use the chicken during the week in hot dishes and then chicken salad.

23 – Freezer Winter Squash Orzo

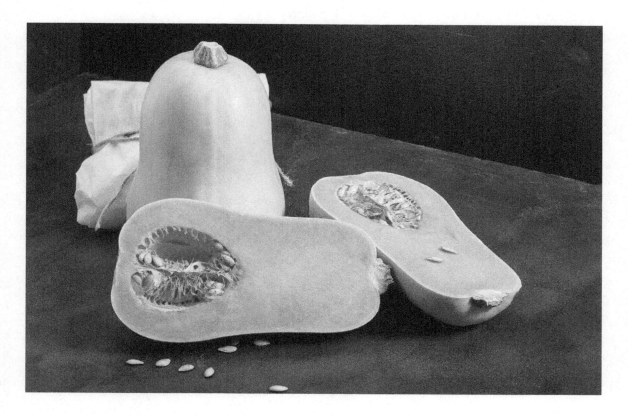

Sometimes, I like having a pasta dish I can make quickly and heat up as needed. This orzo and squash dish fits that bill well.

Makes 6 Servings

Cooking + Prep Time: 1 hour 5 minutes

Ingredients:

- 2 1/2 cups of butternut squash, 1/4" cubed
- 3 tbsp. of oil, olive
- 1/4 tsp. of salt, sea
- 1/4 tsp. of pepper, ground
- 1 cup of orzo pasta, whole wheat or regular
- 2 cups of spinach, shredded
- 2 tbsp. of oil, olive
- 1 minced clove of garlic
- 1/3 cup of crumbled blue cheese

Instructions:

1. Preheat the oven to 425F.

2. Toss the squash in 1 tbsp. oil. Spread in one layer on cookie sheet. Bake in 425F oven till squash has started to brown, and is tender, 35-45 minutes.

3. Place spinach in large-sized bowl. Set it aside. In small-sized skillet heat last 2 tbsp. oil till barely warmed. Add garlic and stir it in. Allow it to set till you've prepared remainder of meal.

4. Place orzo in pot. Cover with two inches of water or more. Bring to boil, then reduce to simmer. Cook till tender. Don't let it get mushy, though. Drain orzo. Pour atop spinach. Allow it to sit on spinach to help it wilt a little.

5. Add squash to pasta. Add garlic-infused oil and blue cheese. Toss till combined well.

6. Transfer individual servings to food containers. Freeze till ready to use. Microwave for 1-2 minutes to reheat.

24 – Make Ahead Ricotta Spinach Rotolo

This is not a well-known pasta dish, but it's very tasty. It normally takes a while to prepare, but the version is baked, which means it's easier to make.

Makes 5+ Servings

Cooking + Prep Time: 1 hour 20 minutes

Ingredients:

- 8 to 10 lasagna sheets, fresh
- 1 cup of shredded mozzarella cheese
- 1 tbsp. of oil, for later, to drizzle

For filling

- 1 pound of frozen/thawed chopped spinach
- 1 pound of cheese, ricotta
- 1 cup of shredded mozzarella cheese
- 1 egg, large
- 1/2 cup of shredded Parmesan cheese
- 1 grated clove of garlic
- 1/4 tsp. of grated nutmeg
- 3/4 tsp. of salt, kosher
- 1/2 tsp. of pepper, black

For sauce

- 2 tbsp. of oil, olive
- 2 minced cloves of garlic
- 1/2 diced onion
- 3/4 tsp. of salt, kosher
- 1/2 tsp. of pepper, ground
- 24 oz. of tomato puree, no salt added
- 1 1/2 cups of water, filtered

Instructions:

1. To prepare sauce, heat oil in oven-proof, 10-inch skillet on med-high.

2. Add the garlic. Sauté for 8-10 seconds.

3. Add onions. Cook till translucent. Add tomato paste, filtered water, chili flakes, kosher salt ground pepper.

4. Simmer mixture for five to seven minutes over med-low. Stir in basil. Scoop out reserve a cup of tomato sauce for serving. Keep the sauce warm.

5. To prepare the filling assemble, preheat the oven to 350 degrees F.

6. Place all ingredients for filling in large bowl. Use a wooden spoon to mix thoroughly.

7. Lay out lasagna sheet with short end facing you.

8. Place 1/3 cup of packed filling on sheet of lasagna. Dab water on furthest end from you, sealing the roll. Start with end facing you and roll lasagna up. Finish with seal facing down.

9. Cut the rolls into threes. Place smaller rolls in tomato sauce. Filling side should face up.

10. Repeat those steps with remainder of lasagna sheets till you have used up all the filling.

11. Drizzle tomato sauce reserved earlier over lasagna, but do not completely cover.

12. Use foil to loosely cover and bake in 350F oven for 1/2 hour.

13. Remove from the oven and uncover. Drizzle with some oil and top using mozzarella cheese.

14. Return to oven and bake for 15 minutes, till cheese is golden and bubbly.

15. To make this dish ahead, use steps up to baking, but freeze first and bake when you're ready to use. Cool tomato sauce and add 3/4 cup of water. Stir. This is to hydrate the sheets of lasagna when frozen. Assemble dish but leave cheese off. Freeze in airtight container. Defrost completely when ready to use. Bake for 40 minutes covered, then add cheese bake for 15 minutes more.

25 – Freezer Ham Cheese Hot Pockets

These hot pockets are freezer friendly and a home-made, healthy alternative to buying Hot Pockets® at the store. You may possibly have some of the ingredients at home, including ham and cheese and olive oil.

Makes 8 Servings

Cooking + Prep Time: 2 hours 20 minutes

Ingredients:

- 1 tube of dough, pre-made crescent rolls
- 2 1/2 cups of ham
- 1 1/2 cups of cheese, mozzarella
- 1 1/2 cups of cheese, cheddar

Instructions:

1. Preheat the oven to 450F.

2. Lay out one full piece of crescent roll dough at a time.

3. Add meat and cheese. Fold over, making a 1/2-circle shape.

4. Seal edges. Make remainder of pockets.

5. Lay hot pockets on cookie sheet. Then, bake in 450F oven for 12 to 15 minutes.

6. To make ahead, after you bake the pockets, wrap them in cling wrap. Place in freezer-safe zipper top plastic bag. Freeze.

7. To reheat right out of the freezer, unwrap cling wrap and cover hot pocket in paper towel. Place in the microwave for 1 1/2 minutes.

26 – Make Ahead Lentils with Feta Broccolini

The roasted broccolini in this dish is lemony in taste and goes well with the salty feta and lentils. The oil, once spiced, tastes even better than the second or third time around.

Makes 4 Servings +

Cooking + Prep Time: 1 hour 10 minutes

Ingredients:

- 2 tsp. of fennel seeds
- 2 tsp. of coriander seeds
- 1 thinly sliced chile, red
- 2 thinly sliced cloves of garlic
- 1/2 cup + 3 tbsp. of oil, olive
- Salt, kosher
- 1 1/2 cups of picked through, rinsed lentils, green
- 2 bunches of trimmed and lengthwise halved broccolini
- 1/2 de-seeded, thinly sliced lemon
- 3/4 cup of parsley or dill, chopped finely
- 2 tbsp. of vinegar, red wine or sherry
- 4 oz. of sliced feta cheese

Instructions:

1. Preheat the oven to 450F. Grind fennel and coriander seeds.

2. Transfer mixture to small-sized skillet. Add 1/2 cup of oil, chile and garlic. Place on med. heat. Shake pan occasionally while cooking till chile slices slightly shrivel and garlic turns golden brown, five minutes or so. Lightly season spiced oil using salt. Transfer to small-sized bowl.

3. Cook the lentils in large pan with salted, simmering water till tender yet firm, 20 to 25 minutes or so. Drain the lentils. Transfer them to medium-sized bowl.

4. Toss lemon and broccolini on rimmed cookie sheet with last 3 tbsp. of oil. Season as desired. Roast and toss halfway through till lemon has softened and broccolini has charred spots, seven to nine minutes.

5. Pour 1/2 of reserved, spice oil over the lentils. Add vinegar and herbs. Season as desired. Coat by tossing.

6. To make ahead, marinate the lentils without veggies or herbs. Cover and keep chilled till you use them.

27 – Freezer Sesame Honey Chicken Bowls

These handy lunch or dinner bowls offer chicken, veggies and rice with a delectable sticky sauce. They're so easy to enjoy as a healthy meal.

Makes 8 Servings

Cooking + Prep Time: 55 minutes

Ingredients:

- 1 1/2 cups of uncooked rice, white
- 4 tbsp. of oil, olive
- 6 cups of chopped broccoli
- 6 cups of snap peas – trim the ends
- 4 chicken breasts, large – cut in 1" cubes
- Salt, kosher, as desired
- Pepper, ground, as desired
- Sesame Honey sauce, bottled

For garnishing: sesame seeds

Instructions:

1. Cook the rice using directions on package. Divide into eight individual food containers.

2. Heat 2 tbsp. oil in large-sized pan. Add peas and broccoli. Cook for five to seven minutes, till tender and bright green. Add to rice in food containers.

3. Add last 2 tbsp. oil to the pan. Add chicken. Season as desired. Cook for seven to 10 minutes, till cooked fully through. No pink should be seen.

4. Add sauce to pan with chicken. Simmer till it thickens, about two to four minutes.

5. Add chicken to food containers. Drizzle with extra sauce. Use sesame seeds for garnishing if you like.

6. Store food containers in the freezer for four days or less. Serve by reheating.

28 – Make Ahead Chicken Thighs Fennel

Use some extra weekend time to make this meal that creates leftovers built-in. It will make a foundation for meals during your week ahead.

Makes 2 Servings + leftovers

Cooking + Prep Time: 1 1/4 hour

Ingredients:

- 8 finely grated cloves of garlic
- 1 1/2 tsp. of pepper flakes, red, crushed
- 2 tbsp. of honey, pure
- 5 tbsp. of oil, vegetable
- 8 chicken thighs, bone-in, skin-on
- 2 1/2 tsp. of salt, kosher + extra as desired
- 3 de-stemmed, 3/4"-wedge cut fennel bulbs, large – remove fronds
- 8 trimmed scallions
- 1 halved lemon, fresh

To drizzle: sesame oil, toasted

Instructions:

1. Place the racks in middle and upper 1/3 of the oven. Preheat it to 425F.

2. Whisk the pepper flakes, garlic, 2 tbsp. oil and honey in large-sized bowl. Season chicken using 2 1/2 tsp. of kosher salt. Toss, coating in the marinade.

3. Arrange chicken with skin side facing up on cookie sheet lined with baking paper. Allow it to sit outside refrigerator as you are preparing veggies.

4. Toss the scallions and wedges of fennel with last 3 tbsp. oil on separate rimmed cookie sheet. Season using salt. Arrange in one even layer.

5. Roast veggies on the top rack of 425F oven. Roast chicken on the middle rack. Toss the vegetables when half done with 30-40 minute cooking time. Chicken should be browned at 45 minutes and veggies should be softened.

6. Divide the scallions, four thighs and 2/3 of fennel between serving plates. Drizzle using sesame oil. Squeeze 1/2 lemon over the top.

7. To make the dish ahead, transfer the rest of the chicken and all juices from cookie sheet into airtight container. Allow it to cool and chill it. Place remainder of fennel and last 1/2 lemon in separate container. Cover, then chill till you use it.

29 – Make Ahead BBQ Spare Ribs

This is one of my family's favorite make ahead meals. You'll prepare it using country style spareribs; giving you meat that is more tender.

Makes 6 Servings

Cooking + Prep Time: 10 minutes + 6-7 slow cooker hours

Ingredients:

- 2 lb. pork ribs, country-style
- 1 1/2 cups of ketchup, no salt added
- 1 1/2 tbsp. of seasoning, Old Bay
- 1/2 cup of vinegar
- 1/2 cup of sugar, brown
- 1/2 tsp. of liquid smoke

Instructions:

1. Place the ribs in a large zipper top bag.

2. In medium bowl, mix the remainder of ingredients together. Pour the mixture over pork in bag.

3. Next, combine together in the bag. Zip it closed. Label and place in freezer.

4. When you're ready to prepare ribs, remove the bag from freezer. Thaw in refrigerator for about 24 hours.

5. Lastly, pour into slow cooker and cook on low setting for six to seven hours.

30 – Freezer Cobb Salad Lunch Wraps

These wraps include the tastes of a cobb salad, but they wrap neatly for easy eating and portability. They make a great, tasty, filling lunch.

Makes 12 Servings

Cooking + Prep Time: 55 minutes

Ingredients:

- 2 tbsp. of oil, olive
- 2 lb. of chicken breasts
- 1 tsp. of salt, kosher
- 1/2 tsp. of paprika, sweet
- 1 tsp. of garlic powder
- 12 wraps, whole grain
- 3 cups of salad dressing, blue cheese
- 2 heads of washed, dried lettuce, romaine
- 4 cored seeded tomatoes, sliced, medium
- 12 slices of cooked bacon, center-cut
- 4 peeled, then seeded sliced avocados, ripe
- Salt, kosher, as desired
- Pepper, ground, as desired

Instructions:

1. Heat large-sized skillet on med-high. Add 1/2 of oil. Season 1/2 of chicken with 1/2 of paprika, salt garlic powder. Add the chicken to the skillet. Cook for five to eight minutes each side, till done. There should be no pink remaining. Allow to cool and slice.

2. Repeat step 1 with second 1/2 of chicken, oil and spices.

3. Place a whole grain wrap on clean work surface. Spread 4 tbsp. of dressing on the wrap. Place lettuce on top 1/3 of wrap. Top with several tomato slices and 1/2 cup +/- of cooked chicken, 1 bacon piece and several avocado slices. Season as desired. Roll the wrap. Repeat step with remainder of wraps.

4. To make ahead, cut large sized pieces of wax paper. Place wraps on the top of wax paper, one each, and follow instructions for preparing the wraps above. Roll wraps in wax paper when done. Secure with two toothpicks each. Place in freezer in airtight container or zipper top plastic bag till ready to serve.

Conclusion

This cook once eat all week cookbook has shown you…

How to use different ingredients to affect warming, delicious tastes in dishes for the week.

How can you include these recipes in your home repertoire?

You can…

- Make beans farro and smoked sausage pasta, which you have probably heard of them before. They are undoubtedly just as tasty as they sound.
- Make soups and stews, which are widely used as make ahead meals. Find ingredients in meat produce or frozen food sections of your local grocery store.
- Enjoy making delectable meat make ahead dishes, including ribs and beef. Meat is a mainstay in recipes year-round, and there are SO many ways to make it great.
- Make freezer dishes using potatoes and pasta. There is something about them that makes meals more comforting.
- Prepare make ahead meals like honey sesame chicken and sweet potato onion wraps. They're sure to be a hit!

Enjoy these mouthwatering recipes with your family and friends!

About the Author

Allie Allen developed her passion for the culinary arts at the tender age of five when she would help her mother cook for their large family of 8. Even back then, her family knew this would be more than a hobby for the young Allie and when she graduated from high school, she applied to cooking school in London. It had always been a dream of the young chef to study with some of Europe's best and she made it happen by attending the Chef Academy of London.

After graduation, Allie decided to bring her skills back to North America and open up her own restaurant. After 10 successful years as head chef and owner, she decided to sell her business and pursue other career avenues. This monumental decision led Allie to her true calling, teaching. She also started to write e-books for her students to study at home for practice. She is now the proud author of several e-books and gives private and semi-private cooking lessons to a range of students at all levels of experience.

Stay tuned for more from this dynamic chef and teacher when she releases more informative e-books on cooking and baking in the near future. Her work is infused with stores and anecdotes you will love!

Author's Afterthoughts

I can't tell you how grateful I am that you decided to read my book. My most heartfelt thanks that you took time out of your life to choose my work and I hope you find benefit within these pages.

There are so many books available today that offer similar content so that makes it even more humbling that you decided to buying mine.

Tell me what you thought! I am eager to hear your opinion and ideas on what you read as are others who are looking for a good book to buy. Leave a review on Amazon.com so others can benefit from your wisdom!

With much thanks,

Allie Allen

Made in the USA
Monee, IL
17 December 2020